W9-BFJ-328

The Seven Continents

Australia

by Xavier Niz

Consultant:
Mark Healy
Professor of Geography
William Rainey Harper College
Palatine, Illinois

Capstone press

Mankato, Minnesota

Bridgestone Books are published by Capstone Press,
151 Good Counsel Drive, P.O. Box 669, Mankato, Minnesota 56002.
www.capstonepress.com

Library of Congress Cataloging-in-Publication Data
Niz, Xavier.
   Australia / Xavier Niz.
      p. cm.—(Bridgestone books. The seven continents)
   Summary: "Describes the continent of Australia, including climate, landforms, plants, animals,
political divisions, people, as well as Australia and the world"—Provided by publisher.
   Includes bibliographical references and index.
   ISBN-13: 978-0-7368-5428-3 (hardcover)
   ISBN-10: 0-7368-5428-2 (hardcover)
      1. Australia—Juvenile literature. 2. Australia—Geography—Juvenile literature. I. Title. II. Series:
Bridgestone books. Seven continents (Mankato, Minn.)
DU96.N595 2006
994—dc22   2005018052

Editorial Credits
Becky Viaene, editor; Patrick D. Dentinger, designer; Kim Brown and Tami Collins, map illustrators;
   Wanda Winch, photo researcher; Scott Thoms, photo editor

Photo Credits
Corbis/Paul A. Souders, 16, 20; Royalty-Free, 1; Theo Allofs, 10 (bottom right); Wayne Lawler, 10
   (left); zefa/Frank Krahmer, 10 (top right)
Digital Vision/NatPhotos, cover (foreground), 12 (top left)
Houserstock/Dave G. Houser, 20 (inset)
Map Resources, cover (background)
Peter Arnold Inc./KLEIN, 12 (top right); Martin Harvey, 12 (bottom); Ted Mead, 6 (top);
   WWI/Ted Mead, 6 (bottom)
Photo courtesy of PJ's Underground/Peter and Joanne Pedler, 18

Table of Contents

Continents of the World

Australia

The world's smallest continent, Australia, is located south of the **equator**. Because of its location, Australia is often called the land down under. This landmass is just a little smaller than the United States. Australia covers almost 3 million square miles (7.8 million square kilometers).

More than 20 million people live on this continent. Australians enjoy the warm **climate** and the unique plants and animals that make up the land down under.

◄ Ocean water surrounds Australia. This continent is not connected to any of the other continents.

Climate

Northern Australia has a **tropical** climate all year. This hot area has a wet and a dry season. During the wet season, about 60 inches (152 centimeters) of rain falls. But the most rain falls along the east **coast**.

Australia's middle, made mostly of **deserts**, is the driest part of the continent. Called the Outback, this area gets less than 10 inches (25 centimeters) of rain yearly.

Southern Australia has a mild climate, with warm summers and cold winters. Most areas get more rain than the Outback.

◄ Australia's climate ranges from wet, tropical northern areas to dry deserts in the Outback.

Landforms of Australia

ARAFURA SEA

INDIAN OCEAN

PACIFIC OCEAN

GREAT BARRIER REEF

GREAT DIVING RANGE

GREAT SANDY DESERT

GIBSON DESERT

SIMPSON DESERT

GREAT VICTORIA DESERT

Darling River

Murray River

Mt. Kosciusko
7,310 feet
(2,228 meters)

AUSTRALIAN ALPS

LEGEND

▲ Highest point

Mountains

⌒ River

N
W E
S

TASMAN SEA

8

| 0 | 200 | 400 | 600 | 800 | 1000 | Kilometers |

| 0 | 200 | 400 | 600 | Miles |

Landforms

In the east, the Great Dividing Range towers over Australia's flat land. These tall mountains separate the wet east coast from the rest of Australia's dry land.

Australia's most important rivers begin on mountains. The Darling River flows from the Great Dividing Range to join the Murray River, which begins on the Australian Alps.

Little water flows in the deserts that cover western Australia. The Great Sandy, Gibson, and Great Victoria Deserts are found there.

Plants

Tall trees grow along Australia's wet north and east coasts. Palm and fig trees cover the tropical north. Tree ferns grow in the rainy climate of the east coast.

Eucalyptuses, Australia's most common trees, grow throughout the continent. They grow tall in wet areas, but are short in dry areas.

In the dry western deserts, tough grasses and shrubs may go months without rain. When it does rain, colorful flowers bloom.

◀ Eucalyptus trees rise above Australia's land (left). Palm trees cover tropical areas. Flowers bloom in deserts.

Animals

Australia is home to many unique animals. These animals roam freely only in Australia. Kangaroos hop across deserts, while koalas sleep in eucalyptus trees. These and other **marsupials** live only on this continent. Australia's emus can't fly, but these large birds can run fast.

The Great Barrier Reef is home to thousands of unique sea creatures. Located off Australia's east coast, it is the largest coral reef in the world. Here colorful rabbitfish swim past giant clams.

◄ Kangaroos and emus live in most areas of Australia. But koalas only live in the east and southeast.

States and Territories of Australia

INDIAN

OCEAN

PACIFIC

OCEAN

NORTHERN
TERRITORY

QUEENSLAND

WESTERN
AUSTRALIA

SOUTH
AUSTRALIA

NEW
SOUTH WALES

AUSTRALIAN
CAPITAL
TERRITORY

VICTORIA

N

W   E

S

Kilometers

0   200   400   600   800

0   100   200   300   400   500

Miles

TASMANIA

States and Territories

Australia is the only continent that is one country. It is divided into six states. Western Australia is the largest state. The smallest state, Tasmania, is an island located to the southeast. Sydney, Australia's largest city, is located in New South Wales.

Australia also has two **territories**. About 300,000 people crowd into the tiny Australian Capital Territory. The large Northern Territory, with many dry desert areas, is home to about 200,000 people.

Population Density of Australia

People per square mile		People per square kilometer
Less than 2		Less than 1
2 to 25		1 to 10
25 to 125		10 to 50
125 to 250		50 to 100
More than 250		More than 100

People

Australia is the least populated continent, except for Antarctica. Twenty million people live in Australia. Most Australians live in cities near the southeastern coast.

Aborigines were the first Australian people. Europeans began moving to Australia in the 1700s. Today, European language and religion are a big influence on this continent. Christianity is the main religion. Australians speak a version of English called Strine. Some Australians still speak Aboriginal languages. Today, about 20 of these languages are used.

◄ These school children (top), and most Australians, live along the southeast coast.

Living in Australia

Most Australians live in apartments or houses. Many houses include an outdoor area for having a **barbecue**. At barbecues, Australians cook meat and seafood on grills.

Australians wear clothes that match the climate they live in. In the tropical north, they wear loose colorful clothes. In the south, people wear T-shirts and shorts during the summer. During the colder winter, they wear warm pants and jackets.

◀ An Australian couple prepares for a barbecue.

Australia and the World

Around the world, people wear jewelry and use coins made from Australia's **minerals**. Many of the world's opals and diamonds, and much of the silver are mined in Australia.

Australia's effect on the world can be seen in many other areas. People visit Australia's Sydney Opera House to watch operas and ballets. Australians' love of water sports has also drawn attention worldwide. Australia has some of the world's best surfers, swimmers, and sailors.

◀ Miners work underground to find opals. Later, many opals are cut, polished (inset), and made into jewelry.

Glossary

barbecue (BAR-buh-kyoo)—an outdoor meal or party
   in which food is cooked using a grill

climate (KLYE-mit)—the usual weather in a place

coast (KOHST)—land that is next to an ocean or a sea

desert (DEZ-urt)—a very dry area of land; deserts receive
   less than 10 inches (25 centimeters) of rain each year.

equator (i-KWAY-tur)—an imaginary line around the middle
   of earth halfway between the North and South Poles

marsupial (mar-SOO-pee-uhl)—an animal that carries
   its young in a pouch

mineral (MIN-ur-uhl)—a substance found in nature that
   is not made by a plant or an animal

territory (TER-uh-tor-ee)—land under the control of a country

tropical (TROP-uh-kuhl)—hot and rainy

Read More

Sayre, April Pulley. *G'day, Australia!* Our Amazing Continents. Brookfield, Conn.: Millbrook Press, 2003.

Striveildi, Cheryl. *Australia.* A Buddy Book. Edina, Minn.: Abdo, 2003.

Internet Sites

FactHound offers a safe, fun way to find Internet sites related to this book. All of the sites on FactHound have been researched by our staff.

Here's how:

1. Visit *www.facthound.com*

2. Type in this special code **0736854282** for age-appropriate sites. Or enter a search word related to this book for a more general search.

3. Click on the **Fetch It** button.

FactHound will fetch the best sites for you!

Index